AF315858

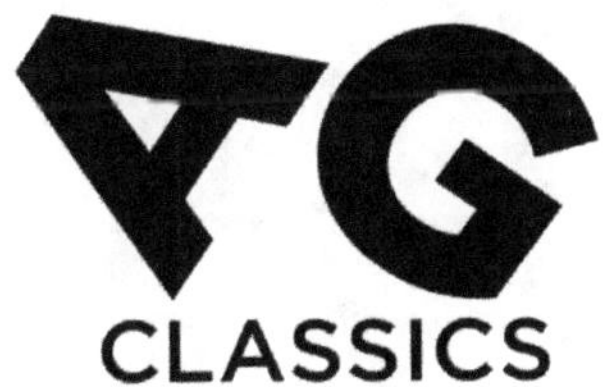

A Schimpflexikon

A Schimpflexikon

H. L. Mencken

Edited by Richard Kostelanetz
Produced by Zachary Zarzycki

FarEast BushWick
AG CLASSICS 2024

An audaciously courageous writer, willing to write what others would not, H. L. Mencken (1880-1956) made a monumentally unprecedented move with his *A Schrimpflexicon* (1928), where he published under his own name a wide variety of negative reviews of himself and his work. The epithet, derived from the German, identifies, roughly, a dictionary of vituperation. Ever the earnest editor, Mencken divided his gatherings into chapters whose titles must be sampled to be believed: Zoölogical, Genealogical, Pathological, as a Truth-Seeker, As a Scoundrel, Miscellaneous Elegances, Winces of the Gailed, and Kosher or Terefah? While publishing under one's own name a book with words all but entirely from other people can be a common move; a book entirely of negative notices became singular. (Reflecting Mencken's influence, I once published some of the dumbest editors' rejection letters to come my way; but since celebrity equal to his has never come my way, negative published reviews of me or my work are scarce.) One paradox of Mencken's career is that the independent critical courage that made him famous during the 1920s became less fashionable in later decades; it's rare today.

–Richard Kostelanetz, from the third edition of his
DICTIONARY OF THE AVANT-GARDES (2018)

MENCKENIANA

MENCKENIANA

A Schimpflexikon

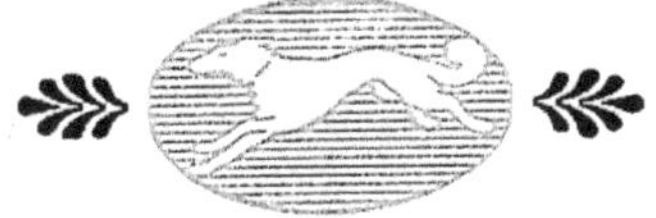

New York

ALFRED·A·KNOPF

MCMXXVIII

Note

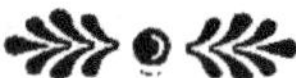

THIS collection is not exhaustive, but an effort has been made to keep it representative. The original materials would fill many volumes: they include hundreds of savage articles and newspaper editorials, and a number of whole pamphlets. During the single year 1926 more than 500 separate editorials upon the sayings and doings of Mr. Mencken were printed in the United States, and at least four-fifths of them were unfavorable. Himself given to somewhat acidulous utterance, he has probably been denounced more vigorously and at greater length than any other American of his

time, not even excepting Henry Ford, Robert
M. LaFollette, Clarence Darrow, and Sacco and
Vanzetti. Here there is room only to offer
some salient specimens of this anti-Mencken
invective—mainly single sentences or phrases,
torn from their incandescent context. Some
were chosen for their wit—for there are palpable hits among them!—, some for their blis-
tering ferocity, and some for their charming
idiocy. The rest of the material awaits the
literary resurrection men of another and perhaps less indignant day.

THE PUBLISHER

Contents

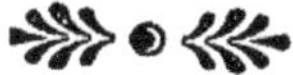

A Schimpflexikon

❧ ● ☙

MENCKENIANA

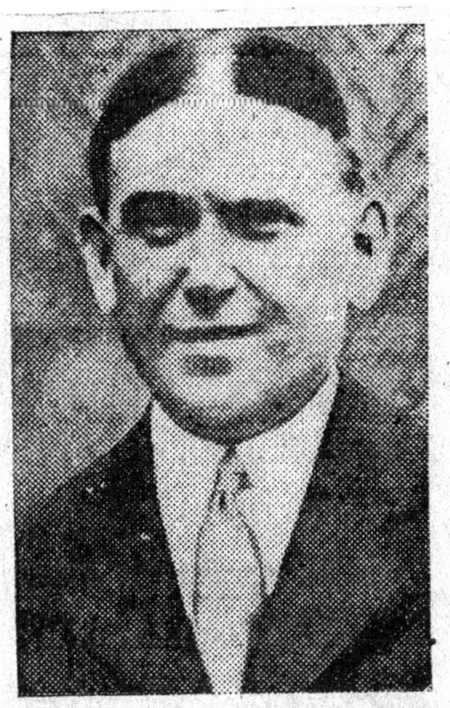

H. L. MENCKEN.

Zoölogical

I WILL content myself with the bald statement
that he is a weasel.

SAMUEL R. GUARD, *broadcasting over* WLS.

THIS MAGGOT, this ghoul of new-made graves,
this buzzard!

EUGENE L. PEARCE, *in the Tampa Times.*

THIS JACKAL in the lion's skin! . . . This tad-
pole of the puddle, grown a toad! . . . Our
comments have been somewhat repressed because the postal regulations forbid the use of
certain adjectives.

The Jackson (Miss.) News.

THE LITERARY man-eating tiger.

The Norfolk Virginian-Pilot.

HE VICIOUSLY attacks and devours such American masterpieces as Lincoln's Gettysburg Ad-

dress . . . as a starving mountain-goat would dispose of a dime-novel.

JAMES M^cSPADDEN, in the Des Moines Register.

COMMON DECENCY would seem to dictate that if Mencken and his ilk regard men of commerce with such high disdain . . . they should hie themselves to some far-distant jungle, there to drown the anthropoidal chatter with sub-simian gabble of their own. While such a step, of course, would be a boon to man, it would be a quite unmerited infliction on the apes.

E. C. W., in the Chicago Post.

A DOG that bites the hand that feeds it.

CLARENCE E. MONSTEELE, in the Camden (N. J.) Courier.

A POLE-CAT.

The San Francisco Chronicle.

A HOWLING hyena.

FREDERICK SULLENS, in the Jackson (Miss.) News.

To FURTHER the mysterious processes and purposes of life such human beings as Lewis and Mencken have their ordained place, together with the jackals and the weeds, the vermin and the microbes.

The Omaha World-Herald.

A YALE professor, speaking at Baltimore, likened Mencken to Paine. Hyperion to a satyr, a royal tiger to a singed cat!

The Raleigh (N. C.) News and Observer.

MENCKEN'S MENTAL tastes remind me of the physical appetite of a sea-gull.

ALLAN T. WEST, *in the Norfolk Virginian-Pilot.*

HIS SORT of journalism reminds me of the flies that gather about the garbage in Summer, and delight in what they can discover.

The Diapason (Chicago).

" PERHAPS," OBSERVES an exchange, " society needs Mencken as Nature needs mosquitoes."

However, it will be observed that we still screen against mosquitoes.

The Philadelphia Inquirer.

SPEAKING OF dogs, our ambition is to own a nice poohpoohdle. Of course we'll call him Mencken.

The New York Herald Tribune.

WITH A pig's eyes that never look up, with a pig's snout that loves muck, with a pig's brain that knows only the sty, and a pig's squeal that cries only when he is hurt, he sometimes opens his pig's mouth, tusked and ugly, and lets out the voice of God, railing at the whitewash that covers the manure about his habitat.

WILLIAM ALLEN WHITE.

WASP AND pole-cat purely!

The Minneapolis Journal.

ONE OF those little skunks who spread their poison wherever they go.

O. B. ANDREWS, *to the American Legion, Chattanooga, Tenn.*

IF MR. MENCKEN would put a photo-spectroheliograph on his ramshackle, tergiversating cerebrum, I think he would discover that he was something of a syentognathous physoclistous levirate levantine belone with perissodactyl affinities; in other words, an acanthopterygian lophobranch not far removed from a plectognathic sesquipedalian orthopter. My opinion of my mendacious friend is summed up briefly in the expressive hemidemisemiquaver, orthorphoitosukohphantodikotalaiporos.

> DR. HOWARD A. KELLY, *of the Johns Hopkins Medical School.*

A PARASITE.

> H. W. STANLEY, *to the San Antonio Kiwanis Club.*

THE LITTLE world outside, we hear, is infested with menckens — "menckens" being a mongrel colloquialism indigenous to these parts, describing an objectionable person and meaning "mangy ape."

NANNIE H. CHESNUTT, in the Nashville Tennessean.

A LITERARY hyena sitting on a hill and laughing at all he beholds.

The Mason City (Iowa) Gazette.

IN THE entire City of Baltimore there is only one who generalizes with such large waving of his ears to make a jackass of himself — and he is it.

The Pittsburgh Post.

COMPARED TO a sound Rotarian from any healthy Main Street in the United States, Mr. Mencken is as a well groomed Pekinese poodle to the majestic St. Bernard of the Pyrenees monks.

The Bellingham (Wash.) Herald.

WHEN THE public cannot see a would-be literary man for the dust, there is always a chance that

he may make himself smelled by turning pole-
cat. H. L. Mencken has pursued the latter course
and the odors he is able to stir up make those of
the Chicago stockyards smell like a tuberose by
comparison.

The Minneapolis Star.

MENCKEN, DISCUSSING any subject, reminds one
of a dog killing a snake. He is foaming, frenzied,
furious.

THOMAS LOMAX HUNTER, *in the Petersburg (Va.)
Index.*

WHEN MR. MENCKEN tries to be humorous he
has all the subtlety and grace of a trick elephant
dancing on an inverted tub.

PERCY A. HUTCHISON, *in the New York Times.*

FROM HIS magazine soapbox an agitator named
H. L. Mencken denounces Americans as " the
boobery." If he means there's no chance of

becoming anything like an H. L. Mencken, we're ready to drop a grateful penny in the monkey's paw.

The Pittsburgh Post.

A MANGY mongrel.

The Iowa Legionaire.

OF SUCH a man [Bryan] most widely known and universally respected in his generation, this human jackal of literary verbosity [Mencken] would slaver and snarl; of such a man, this cynical hyena, without a shred of conscience in his makeup, would raise his shrill cry of derision; of such a man this bloodless vivisectionist would viciously dismember with play of words and phrases and destroy the memory of the honorable American citizen as he lies dead, and strike at him with the fell purpose of destroying the ideals of men and women who believe in something dearer than the beliefs of the Darwins and the Darrows and the Menckens, and all that iconoclastic tribe of scoffers and scorners, who seek to make the world a Godless chaos. We may ask: What has Mr. Mencken done for the world? The winds of time over the deserts of eternity answer: Nothing! " Howl, jackal, the lion is dead! "

The Cascade (Iowa) Pioneer.

A STORMY petrel of unbalanced mental potentialities.

The Cincinnati Inquirer.

MENCKEN IS clever in precisely the same way that a monkey in the park who dances up and down on his trapeze, and simulates human activities, is clever.

The Bridgeport (Conn.) Post.

Mr. Mencken is Zarathustra's contemporary ape.

E. MERRILL ROOT, *in the Measure.*

One can picture Mr. Mencken perspiringly pirouetting above the sawdust arena of a circus, gesticulating behind menagerie-bars to the delight of unambitious groundlings, thumping at the grotesque chautauquas of Lesbian flappers and cuckold clerks.

V. F. CALVERTON, *in the New Leader.*

Genealogical

Mr. Mencken did not degenerate from an ape, but from an ass. And in the process of " revolution " the tail was eliminated, the ears became shorter and the hind parts smaller; but the ability to bray was increased, intensified, amplified and otherwise assified about one million times.

J. B. TEDDER, *in the Chattanooga News.*

The south and Southern literature and social caste have nothing to fear from such as Mencken. There was here an ancient aristocracy when his ancestors dwelt in caves and ate raw meat; there was a civilization here when his grandfather, the gentleman in the dugout, flourished a knotty club, and lived upon the carcasses of wild beasts.

The Little Rock (Ark.) News.

BUT WHO is this influential Mr. Mencken, we ask. And then we answer ourself by saying he is a product of Baltimore, which was, during the reign of the long toddy, the Southern whisky capital, and looked it. From that dingy metropolis Mr. Mencken ramified to New York, the county seat of supermandom.

The Dallas News.

MENCKEN IS descended from the Neanderthal man and the famous Shooting Bull, chief of the Siouxdo Smart sets.

Hearst's Chicago Herald-Examiner.

HE IS either vomiting vitriol because he is paid for it, or he has fed on his own venom until he is reeking with poison which exudes from his perspiration. His name indicates an ancestry which might account for his jaundice.

The Little Rock (Ark.) Methodist.

A DISAPPOINTED, dishonest, distruthful, disgrace-
ful, degraded, degenerate evolute of a species
fifty-seven varieties lower than a turkey buzzard.
God made man and every living creature. Dar-
win made an error. Darrow made a mistake. But,
who in H— made Mencken?

> HOWARD HAMMOND, *in the St. Michaels (Md.)
> Comet.*

PERSONALLY, I should rather be a hill-billy of
the Bible Belt than to have been born with a
silver spoon in my mouth, and that spoon filled
with galvanized gall.

> WIGHTMAN F. MELTON, *in Hearst's Atlanta
> Georgian.*

IN THE not very remote past a wiggle in the
mud got alive, and in the course of time, became maggot, gadfly, cockroach, wasp, tobacco
worm, scorpion, bat, English sparrow, cow-bird,

buzzard, polecat, hyena, jackal, monkey, jack-ass and eventually evolved Mencken.

NANNIE H. CHESNUTT, in the Nashville Tennes-sean.

WE ARE not fully informed as to Mencken's color or race, but his remarks about Negro superiority in the South lead us to believe that he must be a Negro by inclination if not by birth. He is, as a matter of fact, far inferior to the average Southern Negro.

The Tampa (Fla.) Tribune.

THERE IS one thing that must be humiliating to the spirit of the South, and this is the fact that a city of Southern sentiment and ideals such as Baltimore should be charged with being the birthplace of H. L. Mencken. Our sympathy goes out to the great community that was founded in the day of the Calverts.

The Memphis Commercial-Appeal.

MENCKEN, LIKE his great-aunt, Adah Isaacs Menken, is exotic fruit, not good, red meat.

HENRY HELLEN, *in the Chicago Tribune.*

BISMARCK WAS the super-Boche of German *Kultur,* and, as blood will tell, the erstwhile Bright Boy of Baltimore has in time evolved into the super-Boche of our American culture. He has all the family mannerisms.

ALLITERARICUS, *in the St. Louis Mirror.*

A PATRONYMIC with a sinister Hunnish sound.

The Danville (Va.) Register.

Pathological

THE WORLD'S greatest alphabetical mountebank,
perpetually suffering from logomachitis, or
acute inflammation of the stylus. If all he writes
is true, he is a very sick man.

The Step-Ladder (Chicago).

IF MENCKEN only ran about on all fours, slaver-
ing his sort of hydrophobia, he would be shot by
the first policeman as a public duty.

E. F. KEENE, *in the Concord (N. H.) Monitor.*

A CONCEITED kid of the Leopold-Loeb type.

The Buffalo Express.

COME TO Arkansas, Mr. Mencken, and get your
liver drained!

The Arkansas Democrat.

HIS ALCOHOLIC spleen.

CHARLES T. CARPENTER, *in the Kansas City Star.*

HE IS as one vomiting bile at something above him and beyond his capacity to throw up to, so that everything falls back in his face.

Much Ado (St. Louis).

H. L. MENCKEN says the Liberty Bell episode was a myth. That man just naturally can't stand for anything that is more cracked than he is himself.

The Los Angeles Record.

MAYBE THE trouble with Mencken is that he himself resorted to the *Mercury* treatment too late. The doctors of medicine have for years been prescribing copious doses of the quicksilver remedy for a disease that, in the tertiary stage, often manifests itself by locomotor ataxia or paresis. Mencken seems to have fallen a victim to both at the same time, only that in his case there is a lack of co-ordination of thought instead of legs.

> CHARLES PATRICK JOSEPH MOONEY, *in the Memphis Commercial-Appeal.*

HE MUST have a sour stomach.

> *The Akron (O.) Press.*

MENCKEN WAS at his best when his pituitary gland was only slightly affected.

> *The Montana American (Butte).*

A SUFFERER from old-fashioned liver complaint.

> *The Kansas City Journal.*

IT IS a far cry from the cheerful and scintillating Irvin S. Cobb to the morose and bedimmed H. L. Mencken. Mencken is afflicted with a severe attack of mental indigestion.

> *The Atlanta Journal.*

THE GANGRENE of this man.

> W. E. CHRISTIAN, *in the Charlotte (N. C.) Observer.*

PERHAPS MR. MENCKEN suffers from persistent nervous gastritis, or is a victim of pernicious biliousness.

The Montreal Star.

ONE MIGHT, at first thought, believe there was something the matter with his liver, or his kidneys, or his gall-bladder, but on second consideration one realizes the trouble is deeper than that. It's way down in the soul!

WALTER G. SMITH, *in the Kansas City Star*

THE WRITINGS of H. L. Mencken reflect the workings of a disordered intellect.

G. WILLIAMS, *in the Baltimore Sun.*

MENCKEN HAS dysentery of the mouth.

B. C. PAYNE, *in the Daily Oklahoman (Oklahoma City).*

THE BOY-PERVERT from Baltimore.

ARTHUR B. MINIKES, *in the New York University Daily News.*

Freudian Diagnoses

MENCKEN HAS the point of view of one bred in the back of a city lot. He has never traveled. He is essentially a bromide and Babbitt, suffering from an inferiority complex.

DEMOCRITUS, *in the Washington News.*

MR. MENCKEN, that American Loud-Speaker, is suffering from a serious superiority complex.

The Queen (London).

H. L. MENCKEN, the Southern-born anti-Southerner, is out with a base-drum denunciation of all journalists. This makes the list complete; Mr. Mencken has now abused and vilified in the most unrestrained manner every class of mankind of which he is a member. Thus he has drawn a finished picture of the Mencken psychology. He has in so many words announced to all and sundry that he is suffering from a thinly disguised feeling of inferiority and an illy repressed sadistic impulse.

The Asheville (N. C.) Citizen.

THIS NEWER cult of Menckenism harks back ideologically to Nietzsche and not to the Nazarene. The bilious souls, young and old, with the inferiority complex must have their justification and here, at last, they find it in Menckenism.

The Los Angeles Record.

MUST WE admit Mencken's charges against the American boobery? Is there not one single American boob among so many millions of us who can beat Mencken at his own game and expose his superiority pose as a ruse of nature to hide a weakling's heart?

The Fitchburg (Mass.) Sentinel.

𝔓enalogical

THE LEWIS-MENCKEN aggregation comprises the
world's greatest heavyweight self-jolliers. All
we can say at the moment is that we hope they all
choke!

The Fort Worth Star.

THE PERSON we feel most like kicking in the
place providentially provided for that purpose
is H. L. Mencken, with Col. Harvey next in line.

The Columbus (O.) Journal.

MENCKEN OUGHT to be left to stew in his own
juice.

The Arkansas Democrat.

CANNOT AMERICA produce some one who will
knock Mr. Mencken into a cocked hat, or at least
smack his sassy face?

PROFESSOR J. S. BJÖRNSON, *in the Chicago
Tribune.*

WE HAVE many individuals of the Mencken type
in our cities. No attention is paid to them, except
by the police, who occasionally lock them up. It
might be salutary for Mr. Mencken if he were
accorded similar treatment.

The American Canadian (Chicago).

MENCKEN WEEK should be celebrated annually
by placing H. L. Mencken on a flat car in New
York City, and hauling him across the continent
to San Francisco. He eats sauerkraut, thinks
sauerkraut, dreams sauerkraut, worships sauerkraut, writes sauerkraut.

Collier's Weekly.

MENCKEN, WITH his filthy verbal hemorrhages,
is so low down in the moral scale, so damnably
dirty, so vile and degenerate, that when his time
comes to die it will take a special dispensation

from Heaven to get him into the bottommost pit
of Hell.

The Jackson (Miss.) News.

AFTER CALLING Mr. Comstock a " damned fool "
and an " imbecile " and making nasty insinua-
tions hardly fit to print, Mencken says that Comstock is one of his favorite characters, along with
" Frances Willard, Daniel Drew and Brigham
Young " — a grouping of names that merits
Mencken a vigorous kick.

The Franklin (Pa.) Herald.

SOME KIND friend and well-wisher should take a
bedslat to him and make him smart in body as
well as mind.

The Anaconda (Mont.) Standard.

ONE CALVIN COOLIDGE is worth ten thousand
times ten thousand of this Mencken and his kind.
For such as he one feels justified in recommend-

ing a prolonged residence in the country which
Lenin helped to devastate and render uninhabi-
table.

> MRS. ALFRED J. BROSSEAN, *president-general of
> the D.A.R.*

WHAT MENCKEN needs is a good spanking and a
sentence to about one year of the wholesome en-
vironment of a small Middle Western town.

> *The Mendota (Ill.) Bulletin.*

THIS YOUNG man possesses a mania for the dol-
lar that should lead him to the cells of a prison
and to the wearing of the stripes of a convict.

> *The Augusta (Ga.) Herald.*

HE WOULD be right in his element in the councils
of the Soviet — or one of its jails.

> *The Philadelphia Inquirer.*

HE WOULD render a great service to humanity if
he would close his flapping jaw forever and cast

his filth-disseminating magazines into the Atlantic.

The Minneapolis Star.

IF THIS undesirable freak does not fancy the
United States, let him leave the country for the
country's good.

C. E. STONE, *in the Nation.*

I WOULD suggest that such remarks as are made
by H. L. Mencken be brought to the attention of
Congress for the good and welfare of our be-
loved country.

ANTHONY M. HERG, *in the Hartford Courant.*

SHOULD NOT that terrible work of misplaced
energy and learning make every American who
loves his mother tongue seize upon his ax and
breathe hard while looking about for the author
and his " authorities " ? If we had our way Ring
Lardner and H. L. Mencken would get thirty

years on the verbal rockpile, with no Pardon
Board in session during the term.

The Frazee (Minn.) Press.

HERR MENCKEN seems to be afflicted with a fatal
word-bellyache, only to be cured by a descent
into the warmer air of Gehenna. To that region
we cheerfully consign him, with the *Smart Set*
under one arm and " Prejudices " in his good
right hand. And at his change of base everybody
will smile but the Devil.

The Los Angeles Times.

IT IS my purpose to bring his slanders to the attention of every prominent newspaper and civic
organization throughout the South, and further
to see if there is not some recourse in law to
banish him as a pestilential nuisance from the
country he has so contumaciously insulted, and
whose soil his presence contaminates.

CLIO HARPER, *in the Arkansas Writer.*

As a Critic

Mr. Mencken is a typical Hun in his criticism.
The Los Angeles Times.

Too flippant, too egotistical, too bizarre, too shocking, too altogether immoral, too prejudiced, too darn critical.
The Albany Knickerbocker-Press.

H. L. Mencken will never be the constructive critical influence in America that Elbert Hubbard was and always will be.
The Bellingham (Wash.) Herald.

Mr. Mencken is a mountebank of letters, a juggler of words who derives his greatest enjoyment from letting off a pack of rhetorical firecrackers without regard to the thoughts expressed by the words he strings together.
The Nashville Tennessean.

H. L. MENCKEN is the big butter and egg man of books, and the proof of it is that he criticizes literature in terms applicable only to butter, eggs, cheese, rubber and oils.

The Chicago News.

THE GREAT boob-strafer has gone in for musical criticism. If he could keep hokum, pose and flapdoodle out of his writings — such commodities being inserted for the purpose of revenue only, it appears — he would be able to add something constructive to the appalling output of current literature. This he is unable to do. The blah simply will creep in.

The Wichita (Kansas) Beacon.

IF MENCKEN'S effort at literary criticism is the best he can do, he will do well to go back to the Kaiser at Doorn. Each thinks he is divinely inspired — if either is capable of thinking at all.

The Meridian (Miss.) Star.

HE HAS a certain myopic vision and a rich German-American vocabulary, but he is too violent to be humorous and his discrimination coefficient is perfectly represented by the absolute zero.

The Independent.

WITH A culture without beauty, a logic without human allowance, and an articulateness without any understanding of the value of modulation, he goes his untrammelled way, happily unconscious of the fact that critics can be artists.

SHERWIN LAWRENCE COOK, *in the Boston Herald.*

THE TRUE measure of Mencken lies in the fact that he doesn't inspire thinkers.

ROBERT QUILLEN, *in the Davenport (Iowa) Times.*

WE ALSO discover that we dislike Mencken and adore Chris Morley. Why? Because Morley shares our enthusiasm for R. L. S.

The New York Evening Post.

THERE ARE various kinds of literary critics and Mr. Mencken is the worst kind, in that his criticism is intended to attract attention to himself. Those women who know him probably regard him as a conceited but amusing ass.

The Arizona Republican.

A SAFE rule to follow is to inquire very carefully what Mr. Mencken recommends — and then don't read it.

The Square Deal (Maryland Penitentiary).

So FAR as concerns intelligence and education, Mencken could hardly qualify as valet to Dr. Edwin Mims. In his monthly paroxysm, Mencken chatters like an educated parrot, shies at truth, embraces falsehood, and uses up three pages of his magazine to say nothing. If Mencken ever had a constructive thought, it was buried under his peculiar combination of egoism, virus and sarcocol.

The Nashville Tennessean.

MENCKEN HAS no real love of literature; for no man who does not know a poem from a hole in the ground can by any stretch of the imagination be called a critic. He is purely and simply a mustard plaster.

JOHN FARRAR, *in the Bookman.*

WHAT a distressing spectacle a critic can make of himself when he feeds on a diet of raw meat, with a sauce of sewage and vitriol. H. L. Mencken is the worst example of that type.

The Boston Herald.

IN THE legitimate literary world Mencken is a mountebank, a perpetual and preposterous pageant, a rantipole, a vain hysteric raging to and

fro. He is a pariah, an outcast, a literary rene-
gade.

The Jackson (Miss.) News.

H. L. MENCKEN & Company is a commercial
concern specializing in the manufacture of cap-
sule opinions for the immature.

The San Francisco Bulletin.

H. L. MENCKEN is probably as poor a judge of
poetry as exists.

The Columbia (S. C.) Record.

MR. MENCKEN, it has been said, is a critic. In
this we disagree, believing him to be far more a
politician (baffled perhaps in his first youth by a
leaning toward bad poetry).

LOUIS BROMFIELD, *in the Bookman.*

HIS ESSAYS are full of outrageous lapses from
taste, literary and otherwise. His conceit is his
undoing.

The New Statesman (London).

IN EVERY paragraph he uses a German word where an English word would do as well.

The Cleveland Plain-Dealer.

A LITERARY critic should have not only a sense of beauty, but he should also have knowledge, judgment, poise, fairness, sincerity, restraint, and mastery of any subject he discusses. Except for the fact that he lacks all these qualities, Mencken may be rated as a good critic.

WILLIAM SALISBURY, *in the American Parade.*

SOMETIME AGO we sent him a copy of a pamphlet we got out for Brookes More, " Silence and True Love," and we are delighted that in a recent issue of his erotic magazine he said the following: "It's a dull metrical version of Maeterlinck's essay on silence, itself very hard going." We now feel that we should be very much ashamed of anything he might praise, and have therefore struck his name from our list. We believe you will be delighted to read anything he may condemn, and have sent a copy of "Silence and True Love" to you with our compliments. It enjoys an excellent reputation among the truly refined.

THE THRASH-LICK PUBLISHING COMPANY, *Fort Smith, Ark.*

IN THE American world of letters, Mencken occupies much the same position as the yellow newspaper occupies in the modern journalistic world. His stuff is bought and read in the degree that it is radical and rabid.

The Mason City (Iowa) Gazette.

As an Artist

MENCKEN'S " CHARACTERISTIC brilliance " must have blinded my poor, dull vision, for I can see in it nothing but sloppy hogwash. I'll say that as a slinger of uncomplimentary adjectives he has got Billy Sunday hanging on the ropes.

HILL BILLY, in the Detroit Journal.

HIS MANNER is the most tedious employed by any American writer, not excepting Theodore Dreiser, in whose literary dust Mencken is not worthy to walk.

A. L. S. WOOD, in the Springfield (Mass.) Union.

HIS STYLE is that of a trained elephant.

The Toronto Star.

MENCKEN'S OCCUPATION is writing a dismal jargon of Germanized English and making grimaces at the South.

The Atlanta Journal.

Mencken's style at its best approaches the splendor of a Yiddish janitor denouncing a truckman.

> WILLIAM SALISBURY, *in the Salt Lake City Tribune.*

His purple Hearst style.

> *The Kansas City Star.*

And then the style! It begins to affect one like the din of interminable riveting. Is he actually fond of cacophony?

> HENRY HAZLITT, *in the New York Sun.*

Mr. Mencken is no writer at all, but a brick factory.

> *The New Republic.*

His style is inconclusive, trivial, smart-alecky. It is probably the least adequate means that could be devised of discussing, for, instance, Veblen or Emerson or even Sudermann.

> *The Oakland (Calif.) Tribune.*

MR. MENCKEN writes himself down as an intellectual gorilla, a literary jackal feasting at a grave, a self-parading sectional and wordy ass masking in the skin of Brann, whose coarseness he most successfully imitates, but whose style and wit he strives for in vain.

THE HON. MALCOLM RICE PATTERSON, *former Governor of Tennessee.*

MENCKEN IS one of the salon-singers celebrating the freedom of the artist, but is himself the best example of the fallacy of that dogma. He has rediscovered Nero's philosophy of feasting and futility.

The New Masses.

MENCKEN DOES not live his art. It is for him only a political weapon.

JULIA JOHNSTON, *in the Easton (Md.) Star-Democrat.*

Mr. MENCKEN'S prose sounds like large stones being thrown into a dump-cart.

ROBERT LITTELL, *in "Read America First."*

MENCKEN STOLE his literary style from Brann the Iconoclast.

The New London (Conn.) Day.

LACKING THE essential qualifications for the rôle he essays, Mr. Mencken can deal only in boorish vituperation, with a vocabulary borrowed from Billingsgate and the Bowery.

THE REV. HORACE JAMES BRIDGES, *in the Standard.*

MENCKEN'S STYLE is a mixture of cheap sarcasm and bombastic drivel.

MISS STUDENT, *in the St. Louis Times.*

HIS SENTENCES move forward with the violence of a Wagner overture and the formlessness of a rataplan of jazz.

PROFESSOR LEWIS WORTHINGTON SMITH, *of Duke University.*

As an Evangelist

H. L. MENCKEN's idea of Heaven is "laying across a table in a tavern in the Latin Quarter of Paris" or "sleeping on a bar in Santiago de Cuba."

The Nevada Live Wire.

"THE INTELLECTUALS of the class-room are not reading the Bible, but prefer Mencken," said a lady at the Christian Students' Conference. It is strange that any intellectual would prefer sawdust to bread. Such reading will produce its fruit of evil.

The Raleigh (N. C.) News and Observer.

SUCH MATERIALISTS as Dreiser, Lawrence, Mencken and Sinclair Lewis have lost the sense of immortality.

FRANCES NEILL, *in the Santa Ana (Calif.) Register.*

HE ASSUMES that he is the private secretary of
Almighty God.

R. L. BESHERS, *in the Chicago Tribune.*

MR. MENCKEN bawls so ferociously that when
he has finished shouting we feel we have been
for a walk in a gale. This fiery evangelist has
the damnatory instinct better developed than any
revivalist.

S. P. B. MAIS, *in the London Express.*

MENCKEN IS frankly a diabolist.

The Manchester (N. H.) Union.

THE MORE we read of Mr. Mencken the more we
love the Methodist church.

The First Church Review (Evanston, Ill.).

THE IRRELIGIOUS class are very noisy now. They
are conscious only of darkness and ugliness and
filth. H. L. Mencken is their priest.

The Indian Witness (Lucknow).

IF MR. MENCKEN and his sort do not believe in a hereafter that is their privilege. If they are malicious they may wake up in the other world and find themselves in Hell.

The Memphis Commercial-Appeal.

IN ALL the long corridors of H. L. Mencken's contempt for everything in general and American things in particular there is no turning that leads to a way out, to a solution or a hope.

JOHN TEMPLE GRAVES.

THE REAL Mencken is apparently not a theologian, not a man endowed with " spiritual gifts," but, as shown by Goldberg, " a donkey."

O. KIHLSTROM, *in the Truth-Seeker.*

H. L. MENCKEN, the buzzard of American literature, says that " one bold and intelligent editor could save Mississippi from the blight of Fundamentalism." It is only wild-eyed, loud-mouthed jackasses like Mencken who seek to destroy mankind's faith in the fundamentals of Christianity. By cutting through six inches of fat and drilling through four inches of bone one might possibly find Mencken's brain cavity — but he would not discover any grey matter there.

FREDERICK SULLENS, *in the Jackson (Miss.) News.*

H. L. MENCKEN hates and fears Methodism. Incidentally H. and L. are really his initials, but, having been taught that there is "so much" in the way a thing is said or expressed, we concluded to adopt the above form.

The Howard (Kansas) Courant.

AT A time when the world needs religious and moral principles to guide it, it is a shame that writers of the Sinclair Lewis and Mencken type should prostitute their pens in the unholy cause of religious skepticism and agnosticism.

The Boston Herald.

Who is in more imminent danger of hell-fire, the learned theologians for their erroneous translation of the New Testament, or Mencken, who flatly denies the authenticity of a part of the Word of God?

JOHN W. ANGLIN, *in the Memphis Commercial-Appeal.*

MENCKEN IS a pure materialist. He stays close to the ground. His religious opinions carry no weight at all, incapable as he is to take into consideration the spiritual needs of humanity.

LEON DAUDET, *editor of L'Action Française.*

SINCLAIR LEWIS, H. L. Mencken and such writers publish their indecent articles for no purpose but to make a few dirty dollars. The principle is

the same as sellers of impure food or of poisonous liquor. Such men are dangerous — assassi-
nating pure minds and religious beliefs.

J. KEMP WYSHAM, *in the Baltimore Sun.*

MENCKEN HAS established a new religion, Mercurianity, instead of Christianity.

PROFESSOR EDWIN MIMS, *of Vanderbilt University.*

H. L. MENCKEN is devilish and damned.

The Anaconda (Mont.) Standard.

HE ADOPTED blackguardism as a profession, see-
ing in it his best road to fortune.

The Methodist Review.

MENCKEN IS half-baked spiritually.

JAMES B. CONNOLLY, *in Scribner's Magazine.*

THIS INTELLECTUAL nihilist is the chief iconoclast in that sector of the latter-day intelligentsia
which thinks that morals are a nuisance, that

reverence is archaic, that all altruism is a sham. He is a literary cankerworm.

The Grand Rapids Press.

THE ÆSTHETIC criticism represented by the writings of Mr. Mencken is the literary counterpart of religious evangelism. Both reject reason.

The Truth-Seeker.

MR. MENCKEN irritates not so much by what he says as by the almost invariable bad taste of his manner of saying. His megaphoning from his side of the fence does not differ much from that of the foaming evangelists on the other side.

HENRY BELLAMANN, *in the Columbia (S. C.) Record.*

IN THE United States of America, H. L. Mencken is the prophet of that movement for a liberty which means license without shame. He has developed a positive hatred of health.

The Western Christian Advocate.

It SEEMS natural that a man who would entertain Mr. Mencken should poison himself. Menckenism is the way which leads down unto death.

The Knoxville Journal

As an American

H. L. MENCKEN is fully 90% Prussian in all his utterances, and proud of it. His most malignant and persistent sneers are reserved for any American who was active in enmity to Germany and Austria. His own dearest desire is to be like as possible to a native of Berlin or Vienna.

The Boston Transcript.

A BRITISH toady.

The Lowell (Mass.) Sun.

H. L. MENCKEN continues his rabid anti-British diatribes, always tainted with ribaldry.

The American Canadian (Chicago).

MENCKENISM IS anti-American because it does not understand the poetry of America.

JOHN FARRAR, *in the New York Herald Tribune.*

IF MR. MENCKEN is to use your columns to black-guard virtue and sincerity, to slander England and France, and to outrage the best traditions of this State, either seriously or in the delicacy of his native Teutonic humor, you ought editorially to disapprove and refute such outbursts of bilious pro-Germanism.

ARTHUR W. MACHEN, *in the Baltimore Evening Sun.*

THERE ARE many Americans of German descent who are thoroughly American. Mencken is not one of them.

The Minneapolis Journal.

MENCKEN IS an outstanding, disgusting example of what constitutes a poor American.

The Richmond (Va.) Times-Dispatch.

MENCKEN'S FOLLOWERS are fools, hypocrites, morons, Reds, hyphenates, and traitors. You put yourself in the first three classes and smell like the last three by inflicting him upon your readers.

FRANK MILES, in the Chicago Tribune.

MENCKEN IS an offense in the nostrils of all Americans who love the ideals and best traditions of their country. He seems to love the putrid, the sinful, the low, and uses any occasion to air his antipathy to the customs and beliefs of the average American citizen.

HAROLD N. CORIELL, in the New York Herald Tribune.

HE HAS a German soul, although possessed of American citizenship. He has never assimilated Americanism, nor have American institutions assimilated his spirit or stimulated his enthusiasm. Let him go. Let him stay.

The Huntington (W. Va.) Dispatch.

H. L. MENCKEN, in whose veins runs unsullied
the pure blood of Hungary.

The Vancouver (B. C.) Sun.

MENCKEN, OBVIOUSLY of foreign name, is a
treacherous alien sapping at the vitals of America's proudest and most essential institutions, an
indecent buffoon wallowing in obscenity as he
howls with glee.

The New Haven Union.

WHO is he that he has any right to criticise any
American, no matter who?

C. B. LANGSTON, *in the St. Paul Pioneer-Press.*

HE HAS written articles palliative of Alexander
Berkman, Emma Goldman, and Tom Mooney,
as well as Carlo Tresca.

FRANCIS RALSTON WELSH, *in the Congressional
Record.*

By WHAT stretch of the imagination is a man by the name of Mencken and a follower of Nietzsche to be called a representative American? Although this yellow journalist makes merciless sport of the farmer, the laborer, and woman, he pays abjectly slavish homage to the profiteer, the bootlegger, the vice trust, Wilhelm Hohenzollern, and himself.

The Des Moines Register.

Mr. MENCKEN is a good deal disgusted with America, for no known reason except that it does not regard him as highly as he regards himself.

The Dallas News.

EVERY TIME we have jumped onto this contumacious, swaggering, bullying, cowardly hyphenate, some of his dupes, among them several college professors, have informed us Mencken is as good an American as anybody. For him to insist he is an American and boast of his opposition to our cause when the United States was fighting Germany, brands him as the most contemptible type of Kaiserite and proves that anybody who sees any good in him is either an ignoramus or as un-American as he is.

The Iowa Legionaire.

H. L. MENCKEN is a hardened Germanophile. His gods are Bach, Beethoven, Brahms, Frederick the Great, Nietzsche, Goethe, Ludendorff, Wagner, Plato, Shakespeare and George Washington.

EDWARD E. PARAMORE, JR., *in the Bookman.*

MENCKEN IS a former subject of the German Kaiser. President Pettie, of the Arkansas Advancement Association, has asked the Arkansas

Congressmen to make an investigation as to his citizenship.

The Arkansas Democrat.

MIGHT I timidly ask why Mr. Mencken chooses to remain in this country? Emma Goldman left it.

COBB HALL, *in the Chicago Tribune.*

FOR AUGHT we are aware to the contrary, Mr. Mencken is a Prussian, or a Prussian sympathizer. He is a biographer of Nietzsche. He is a special writer on a paper notoriously subsidized by the Kaiser.

The Truth-Seeker.

IF HE and the pusillanimous curs who are backing him are right, then Judas Iscariot should be sainted, and an American shrine should be erected to the memory of Benedict Arnold.

L. L. HAYDEN, *in the Iowa Legionaire.*

As an Intellectual

THERE ARE thousands of men in the South who scrape more brains from under their thumb-nails every morning than Mencken has any idea of in his existence.

Candid Opinion (Prescott, Ariz.).

THE MAZURIAN marsh he calls his brain.

The Macon (Ga.) News.

A CHEEKY word-slinger who has mistaken a puff-ball for a brain.

The Buffalo Express.

THE DRIPPINGS of his noodle vacuum.

The DeQueen (Ark.) Bee.

EVERY MOTHER who cooks a good meal for her children and darns her husband's socks is more intelligent than Mencken.

PROFESSOR FREDERICK WOELLNER, *in the Los Angeles Times.*

MENCKEN IS a master of bullyragging. He doesn't convince you; he rails and tears his hair and paints a sordid word-picture, forcing your sense of decency to prejudice you against whatever he has in hand. The trouble with him is that he is uneducated.

> HUGH R. SMITH, *in the Dove (University of Kansas).*

IF HE ever had a real idea his skull would pop like a rotten pumpkin, but he is never in any danger.

> *The Macon (Ga.) News.*

IN HIS glorious upward progress he acquired instead of the gray matter placed in the skulls of Tennesseans by the Almighty, a composite of slime, mould, bunk, miasma, decay, skunk cabbage, devil's snuff, flapdoodle and Hamburger cheese, blended in minor proportions with razor

extract, stump water and valerian. So biggon,
sooey, scat, shoo!

> NANNIE H. CHESNUTT, *in the Nashville Tennes-
> sean.*

HIS WRITING is the gibberish of an imbecile.

> *The Mason City (Iowa) Gazette.*

MR. MENCKEN's widely read illiteracy enables
him to display his natural parts in a way that
will prove a delight to the brainless intellectuals and a source of innocent merriment to
others.

> LEONARD BACON, *in the New York Evening Post.*

MR. MENCKEN's mind seems bilious, and in need
of a drastic purgative.

> *The Hartford Courant.*

AN 18-KARAT, 23-jewel, 33rd degree, bred-in-
the-bone and dyed-in-the-wool moron.

> J. F. BUSEY, *in the Los Angeles Record*

HOWEVER MUCH longer Mr. Mencken will talk he will not say anything new. He is probably, as human values go, insane.

CHANTICLEER, *in the Independent.*

As a Journalist

H. L. MENCKEN thinks journalism is in a low estate. It sure is wherever Mencken touches it.

The Council Bluffs (Iowa) Nonpareil.

H. L. MENCKEN is very much discouraged over the present output of newspaper men. Perhaps we have all unconsciously absorbed some of the Mencken trend of thought.

The Shamokin (Pa.) Herald.

MR. MENCKEN plays a very safe game in his journalism. He is the cagiest editor of the horn-blowing type the country has seen since Elbert Hubbard. His specialty is attacking groups that cannot, or will not, fight back. His shield is the festive generality. He bawls for " freedom," but persecutes those who do not subscribe to his views. His journalism is cowardly, cheap, blatant, crooked and horribly wordy.

MARLEN PEW, in the Editor and Publisher.

MENCKEN IS adjudged guilty in our mind of posing as a devil of a fellow when he is mostly a very clever newspaper man and no more, having no fundamental education to speak of.

The Lewiston (Maine) Journal.

MENCKEN HIMSELF is a journalist, but he seems above and beyond the cardinal principles enunciated by newspaper men recently in Washington, namely, " truth, decency and fairness." He would rather be different than right. And if fairness gets in the way of something snappy he wants to say, so much the worse for fairness.

The Omaha World-Herald.

As a Truth-Seeker

MR. MENCKEN would be greatly crestfallen to learn that he had for one time by inadvertence told the truth.

> THE REV. NOLAND R. BEST, *executive secretary of the Baltimore Federation of Churches.*

WE HAVE a suspicion that, if we were well acquainted with him, we should want to raise his own language to the nth power before being satisfied that we had done his snivelingness, poltroonishness and ignominiousness the full honors deserved, and imparted the information that he's a dirty liar.

> *The Venango News-Herald (Franklin, Pa.).*

IT WOULD be a reflection on all the liars who ever lived to say that Mencken is a liar.

> *The Tampa (Fla.) Tribune.*

MENCKEN IS a writer who has attained a vogue by the simplest of all methods — assuming the untrue and bolstering it with satire and venom. He delights in controverting all rules of conduct and denying all acknowledged statements of fact.

The Manchester (Iowa) Press.

I CAN only characterize Mencken's attitude as pernicious, unscrupulous and ignorant. It has a mere semblance of truth; but that is embedded in palpable falsehood.

PROFESSOR ROBERT SHAFER, *at the University of Cincinnati.*

IT WOULD only be a mistake to take any notice of this denatured American who has found the trade of knocking his own country and people so much to his taste and profit that he has become noted as a professional knocker, making a specialty of knocking his own nation. We confess our inability to arouse a spark of indignation against the writings of so foul-mouthed and irresponsible a slanderer.

The Knoxville Sentinel.

PROBABLY OF all the writers of the period who put their phrases far above their facts, Mencken is chief. There is hardly a statement Mencken makes about Prohibition or about Law Enforcement that will bear the slightest analysis.

The Des Moines Register.

THE KU KLUX parade accomplished its purpose. Even the master egotist of America and its boss iconoclast, who would, if he were big enough, trample upon the altars of patriotism as a bull of Bashan, whose puny pretense of big words seeks to mock at religion and to sneer at patriotism — even this man, H. L. Mencken, was forced by the grandeur of the thing to pour into his cesspool of putridity a little of the salt of truth.

The Fellowship Forum.

MENCKEN DOES not mean to, but he does tell the truth.

The Muscogee (Mich.) Chronicle.

THE ONE thing I most sincerely do not believe in is Mencken's sincerity.

STRICKLAN W. GILLILAN, author of "Off Again, On Again, Gone Again, Finnegan."

MENCKEN WOULD rather wound, and lie to wound, than to heal and be truthful about it.

The Council Bluffs (Iowa) Nonpareil.

FROM THE first word to the last his criticism is utter falsehood.

The New York Commercial.

As an Editor

I_F ANYONE will send me the *Mercury*, I will in-
spect Mr. Mencken's pus collections, but I refuse
to be salivated at my own expense.

JOHN HIGGINBOTHAM, in the Springfield (Mass.)
Union.

M_{ENCKEN} HAS catered to the lowest types of
Americans as well as to the so-called intelligentsia, who ought to know better than to read
the filth he puts out in his green-covered magazine. His appeal has been to the derelicts of society, who, by their very acts, have cut themselves off from decent folk and are at war with
the society which will no longer tolerate them.

H. C. CONNETTE, in the North China Star (Pekin).

T_{HIS} PUTRID public pest, H. L. Mencken, is a
significantly named public nuisance. His initials

are H. L., meaning the first and last of the word Hell. He publishes a magazine called the *American Mercury,* and any doctor will tell you that nobody takes mercury but degenerates who have acquired the most loathsome social sexual disease known after an illicit honeymoon with some unwashed Lazar or Lazarette of the highways.

The Yellow Jacket.

ALL ANYONE has to do to make the columns of Mencken's *Mercury* is to cultivate a wholesouled antipathy for this country, its government, institutions and social customs which they are able to put into language sufficiently insulting to make an honest citizen start in at one end of a ten-acre lot and kick them out of the other.

The Philadelphia Inquirer.

READ MENCKEN *passim,* especially his " Americana " department of monthly rakings by means of clipping bureaus from the entire press of America, with everything winnowed out save those scraps that tend to belittle our civilization. One Mencken in a generation is positively all that we can endure.

PROFESSOR FRED LEWIS PATTEE, *in the Christian Advocate.*

AN EMBITTERED artist once painted a picture of a vampire nobility sucking the blood of a wretched, starving world of workers. There now exists a heartless, barren aristocracy of intellect, the Mencken breed, who fly under the colors of the Green Book. They live by the labor of those they deride. Yet they add no whit of comfort, no mote of beauty, no chord of harmony to the world.

FRANK SOUTHARD, *in Manuscript (Pomona College).*

MERCURIANITY IS the name of a new religion, the Bible of which is a green-covered monthly magazine. Its followers include blasé disciples of Bohemianism; young people in college who believe that anything which tears down is good; seekers after literary and æsthethic thrills, and a host of men and women who are discontented with contemporary American culture.

THE REV. LOUIS I. NEWMAN, *of San Francisco.*

IF THE morals of the barnyard are the morals of America, and the manners of the feeding-trough are the manners of America, and if George S. Viereck and Grover C. Bergdoll are fine outstanding examples of American patriotism, then the *American Mercury* is thoroughly American.

The Bridgeport (Conn.) Telegram.

THE SAIL which was the *American Mercury* turns out to be a catboat. Editor Mencken acquired his fame by being the Jeremiah of American literature, but in the *Mercury* the voice of Jeremiah is silent and the result is a book as staid as the *Atlantic Monthly* and not as interesting.

The Springfield (Mass.) Union.

WE HAVE only one suggestion to make: drop the second word from the title of the magazine.

The Methodist Board of Temperance, Prohibition and Public Morals.

MENCKEN, FREQUENTLY referred to as H—l, literary poseur and self-elected immortal, editor of the *American Mercury,* a publication that is usually handed around with fire tongs, probably would be grieved to the very pit of his stomach if he could realize how unoriginal his remarks about Sister Aimée McPherson are.

The Mountain View (Calif.) Leader.

A TEACHER at one of the great Chicago universities said: " The one thing that makes me fear for the future is the number of our students who read the *American Mercury*. On the campus, you can see copies of it under every arm. Not only do they read it, but they absorb everything it says — they live with it. It is the greatest single danger that exists in American life today."

FLORA WARREN SEYMOUR, in the Step-Ladder.

H. L. MENCKEN, editor of the *American Mercury*, is known in New York as one of its brightest men. He is also openly, notoriously and positively its meanest. He makes meanness pay. Nothing is sacred to Mencken, from the character of George Washington to the divine form of beautiful woman.

The Idaho Statesman (Boise).

HIS ORGAN, the Greenbacked Monster, aims to be a corrosive sublimate magazine, a mordant mixture of mockery, malice, and mendacity.

The Methodist Review.

THE EDITOR of perhaps the worst magazine in the United States.

The Concord (N. H.) Monitor.

As a Statesman

A RADICAL crack-brain.

The Huntington (W. Va.) Herald-Dispatch.

HIS THINKING is the mere indigestion of capitalism. He and his coterie are more dangerous and more reactionary than such crude obstacles to progress as militarists, chambers of commerce, and Ku Klux Klans.

The Milwaukee Leader.

A RADICAL Red. It's a wonder decent people haven't risen up and lynched him.

THE REV. LINCOLN MCCONNELL, *in the Oklahoma City News.*

MR. MENCKEN carries the Hamiltonian disgust with the people to the highest power, and from his little throne looks down upon what he regards as inferior people.

WILLIAM JENNINGS BRYAN.

H. L. MENCKEN is probably the most subtle political propagandist serving the interests of the Democrats.

The Okmulgee (Okla.) Times.

DEMOCRACY IS not only derided in this country, but a smart, flippant and cockawhoop writer like Mencken gets paid for deriding it.

The Springfield (Mass.) Republican.

PARLOR PINKS like Mencken and Brisbane.

The Winston-Salem (N. C.) Sentinel.

EVEN AT this late date, when he has reached the age of forty-five and has never married, there is chatter abroad in the land that he will be a pro-German candidate for President of the United States. Why not?

The Biblio.

H. L. MENCKEN might be a good selection for the cohorts of Antichrist, his platform favoring five-cent beer, the Binet-Simon test for Cabinet members, the abolition of Methodists, compulsory reading of Nietzsche in the public schools, and the shifting of the national capital to Baltimore.

The Hartford Times.

H. L. MENCKEN's " Notes on Democracy " is the most savage of all his savage books. He proceeds, with his usual disemboweling process, to rend democracy to the vitals. Gore flows freely. Mencken, rubbing his bloody hands, breaks into cackles of titanic laughter.

The Miami Herald.

I CAN imagine nothing finer than a government headed by H. L. Mencken and a group of lads who wear soiled linen and think in terms of soiled thought.

E. P. S., *in the Philadelphia Public Ledger.*

THE TIME has not yet arrived when the policies of this country are dictated by the Menckens, the Debses and the LaFollette, Jrs.

Resolution of Hanford Post, American Legion, Cedar Rapids, Iowa.

PRETENDING TO be critical of the more superficial inconsistencies of capitalism, Mencken is one of its staunchest defenders. He tells many lies and many more platitudes.

The Worker (Chicago).

H. L. MENCKEN as Postmaster-General would be a marvel. In that position he could make his literature as obscene as his degenerate mind might dictate and inflict it upon the people to his heart's content.

The Iowa Legionaire.

As a Voluptuary

CAN'T YOU picture him sitting back in the spooners' section of a movie-house, coining smutty remarks about young girls, and other senile indoor sports such as the gaitered dodderers of New York's fleshpot district do to keep up the tempo of their sluggish circulations?

FIFTEEN MEMBERS OF A NATIONAL SORORITY, UNIVERSITY OF CALIFORNIA, in the Los Angeles Record.

LIKE NIETZSCHE and Schopenhauer and other weaklings who wrote ferociously and trembled, Mencken affects to regard the glorious bodies of women as objects of contempt. Reading such passages, one realizes that for this acrid American critic the grapes of womanhood are sour.

The Sporting Times (London).

HERR MENCKEN says that he is tired of having men's secretaries call him up and tell him to wait until Mr. So and So can talk to him. Perhaps Mr. Mencken would prefer to talk to the secretaries without interruption.

The Newport Telegraph.

AND JUST to think that we have with us today the fire-eating Mr. Mencken, in person and wearing red pants! Whoopee! It is to laugh! The bunco-buster become a parlor Bolshevik! How the mighty have fallen! What now, Mencken, has erotic vanity claimed you for its own? Has Cæsar fallen victim to the perfumed enchantments of the salon?

ALLEN V. PEDEU, *in the Houston Post.*

SOME ONE has said that Mr. Mencken shuts up like a clam whenever women or anything about the fairer sex are mentioned. What a rest it would be, what a craved interim from the jargon he pours into our minds, if some kind philanthropist or humanist would invent a miniature woman that would hang constantly before him.

CARL KNOEDLER, in the Chattanooga Times.

SEVERAL AUTHORS have broken into the news lately. H. L. Mencken does it by getting engaged, thus showing that somebody is inclined to take him seriously.

The Boston Herald.

THE MENCKENS are accustomed to trafficking in morasses of racy French literature. They have attained that peak of rarefied highbrowism where the palate quickens only upon highly-seasoned eroticism.

The Louisville Courier-Journal.

MENCKEN IS no battler for real intellectual freedom, as distinguished from freedom to imbibe, freedom to be scurrilous, freedom to be erotic.

The Minneapolis Tribune.

H. L. MENCKEN and Sinclair Lewis believe that life is not worth living unless it can be lived where sewer gas pollutes the atmosphere.

The Miami Herald.

THE LIBIDINOUS hedonism of strict Menckenism.

The New Age (London).

THE Y. M. C. A. teaches a young man healthy fun rather than the lewd and suggestive thoughts that Mr. Mencken seems so eager to champion.

The Muscogee (Okla.) Times-Democrat.

OPPOSED TO Edith O'Shaughnessy, Margaret Wilson, Edna Ferber and E. Barrington, who are genuinely sympathetic in their presentation of character, are the masters of sarcasm, confusion and mechanistic ideology, notably Scott Fitzgerald, Owen Johnson, Sinclair Lewis, H. L. Mencken and Joseph Hergesheimer. Some of the latter have been pictured in the act of smoking. I am not making an anti-nicotine crusade, but I think smoking in a portrait is very like chewing gum or picking one's teeth.

HELOISE E. HERSEY, *in the Boston Transcript.*

MENCKEN SOUGHT to imitate Lord Gordon Byron, of England, who took to a policy of indecency in both his private life and in his work to shock his native land into a recognition of the importance of his ego.

The Chattanooga News.

As a Scoundrel

MENCKEN'S ATTACK on the late Robert Louis Stevenson was the vilest and most cowardly of its kind I have ever read. I feel satisfied that Mencken is the type of man that would take great pleasure in telling the tiny tots on Christmas eve that Santa Claus is a fake and a delusion.

DE MORTUIS NIL NISI BONUM, *in the Chicago Tribune.*

WHAT CAN be said of a man like Mencken who, in the presence of the broken body and spirit of the still living Woodrow Wilson, could refer to him frequently as " the late Woodrow " ?

PROFESSOR EDWIN MIMS, *in the Santa Monica (Calif.) Outlook.*

Kosher or Terefah?

MR. MENCKEN is a clever and bitter Jew, in whom a very real love of letters is everlastingly exasperated by the American love of cheap pathos and platitude. His philosophy is the sort of nihilistic pride which belongs to a man with a sensitive race and a dead religion.

G. K. CHESTERTON.

HE APPEARS to be a Jew of the " dirty bird which fouls its own nest " variety, probably acting in this manner to show that he is different and of finer clay than his fellows.

The American Israelite.

IF H. L. MENCKEN, the well-known mocker and derider of current civilization, is, as alleged, a descendant of Haym Salomon, that is monument enough for Haym.

E. S. MARTIN, *in Life.*

Away with the inhibition of inferiority this clever Hebrew would wish upon us!

ARABELLA JAMESON, *in the Raleigh (N. C.) News and Observer.*

A NATIONALITY which has raised itself from poverty to wealth in a single generation, a race which has produced such great men as Oscar Straus, Louis Brandeis, Adolph Ochs and Rabbi Wise, have reason to be thankful that a carping critic such as Mencken can lay no claim to their nationality.

The Madison (Wis.) Courier.

ABJECT SERVILITY to the Pope explains the yellowness of many so-called American newspapers and why so much space is found available for the slanderous ravings of the Mencken-type buzzards of journalism.

The Fellowship Forum.

A JEWISH expert screwing the microscope into his jaundiced eye, and shaking his head over all the jewels proffered in America by Americans.

The Montana American (Butte).

MENCKEN IS connected with the New York *World*, the attitude of which toward Romanism and Rum the reader should know full well. From his name, he seems to be a Jew, or at least a German, and recently in an Alabama daily he was sneering at Genesis.

The Alabama Christian Advocate.

Ex-Cathedra

You can bet your life I was not raised on Mencken and bridge parties. I got my faith from the hickory stick.

THE REV. HILLYER HAWTHORNE STRATON, *of New York.*

Mencken classes the Methodists and Baptists with the Ku Klux because of the high idealism of these denominations.

THE REV. C. R. JENKINS, D.D., *of Macon, Ga.*

Let us adopt the Bible as a text-book of literature, history, philosophy and religion in the public schools to combat the destructive influence of that foul-minded satyr, H. L. Mencken. Christian public school educators today are crying to the churches for help in combating the menace of Menckenism.

THE REV. HENRY EDWARD TRAILLE, D.D., *of Seattle.*

MENCKEN IS the foremost American example of Nietzsche's "superman." He is this country's greatest single exponent of materialism and of enmity to religious forms and observances. He has no regard for truth.

THE REV. NELSON S. GARDNER, *of Wichita, Kansas.*

WITH NO word of praise for Negro poets or composers, Mr. Mencken takes a dastard fling at the colored pastor. He could not hide his cloven foot.

THE REV. JOHN W. ROBINSON, D.D., *of New York.*

H. L. MENCKEN is in the forefront of the dishonest writers and clever liars who would debauch a wholesome and helpful humanism and lead the modern world astray.

THE REV. LYNN HAROLD HOUGH, D.D., *in "Evangelical Humanism."*

A BARNSTORMING fanatic.

> THE REV. ROBERT H. MACNAIR, D.D., *of Kansas City.*

WHY, I tell you folks, Mencken is just a dirty buzzard and the folks that follow him are no more than damn scoundrels.

> THE REV. LINCOLN MCCONNELL, D.D., *of Oklahoma City.*

MENCKEN APPEALS to bootleggers, street walkers and the like.

> THE REV. MILO E. PEARSON, D.D., *of Lewiston, Maine.*

MR. MENCKEN'S tirade is irresponsible bluster, vacuous and malicious balderdash. His war-time propaganda was, to put it mildly, not above suspicion. His pseudo-opposition to the Klan is revealed to be merely another ill-concealed attempt to aid and abet the enemy — by indirection.

> THE REV. HUGH PENDLETON MCCORMICK, D.D., *of Baltimore.*

H. L. MENCKEN and Sinclair Lewis, and all their thorny tribe, were meant for Isaiahs and Ezekiels and St. Pauls. They crawl away into their libraries to snarl and carp and bite because they did not, at some crucial moment in their careers, learn to worship and confess and transform the life about them with spiritual forces.

THE REV. SAMUEL M. SHOEMAKER, D.D., *of New York.*

LET US not be troubled over the Sinclair Lewises or the Menckens, over slanders and lies, over sneers and ridicule, over the bitter hatred of Methodism by the bootleggers and boozers. The answer to them is a pure ministry and a holy church.

THE REV. W. D. MARSH, D.D., *of Potsdam, N. Y.*

TO PASS by and resume ignoring our cousin, the Anglican anabissinian, we discover ourselves the victims of a native simulacrum in the person of that Baltimorean buttinsky, H. L. Mencken. The lunacy in Mencken is that he imagines that his Maryland " diamond-back " brain is the laboratory of a new pansophy.

THE REV. SAM W. SMALL, D.D., *of Atlanta.*

MENCKEN LIVES down on the low class of vulgarity and he thinks everything else is vulgar.

THE RIGHT REV. E. D. MOUZON, D.D., *of North Carolina.*

PASTORS AND orators should talk to the students, and those overfed and underworked youths should be steered into the path of religion and the church, and be saved from the beliefs preached by H. L. Mencken and his ghoulish crowd.

THE REV. S. PARKER CADMAN, D.D., *president of the Federal Council of Churches of Christ in America.*

I CAN understand how the moron-minded might approve Mencken or even admire him, but how any mortal man with a capacity to think at all could profess "*profound* admiration" for one so superficial is beyond comprehension!

THE REV. JOHN ROACH STRATON, D.D., *of New York.*

WE CAN get a delightful close-up of the Higher Hooliganism in the person of one of its corps commanders, H. L. Mencken. Mencken is the Peck's Bad Boy of American literature. His ideas on things American express superbly the Teutonic view of politics, morals, women, beer and literature.

THE REV. HALFORD E. LUCCOCK, D.D., *in the Christian Advocate.*

ONE H. L. MENCKEN, whose name sounds like that of a German, Polish or Russian Jew, said to be foreign-born and a product of the schools of

Germany, has sneeringly called the South the Bible Belt.

THE REV. JAMES M. GLENN, D.D., *in the Birmingham (Ala.) Christian Advocate.*

WHAT CHEAP blatherskite of a pen-pusher can refer to courage while he is a guest of the Great Volunteer State? None but a nut suffering with a severe case of Menckenitis. Let your gourd-seeds rattle, buddy; they don't sprout! We are accustomed to sending the police to investigate when a stranger is seen sneaking around like this. I hereby invite him to come out and get acquainted with some real American citizens. One of them will be a Baptist preacher.

THE REV. A. C. STRIBLING, D.D., *of Dayton, Tenn.*

NOT A few youths of the present generation seem to think it is smart to dispose of God in a wise crack, to impale goodness on the point of an epigram. In poetry it is symbolized by Omar Khayyam, in drama by George Bernard Shaw, in fiction by Michael Arlen, in magazine literture by H. L. Mencken and his *American Mercury.*

> THE REV. HERBERT A. JUMP, D.D., *of Ann Arbor, Mich.*

THE THINGS Mencken writes are awful!

> THE REV. DANIEL A. POLING, D.D., *president of the United Societies of Christian Endeavor.*

H. L. MENCKEN pours forth denunciation in bitter, vulgar language upon the illustrious dead. The expression from this Mencken indicates his appalling degeneracy. They indicate a creature devoid of decency or truth. That he lives in Baltimore is to Baltimore's disgrace.

> THE REV. CHARLES E. JONES, D.D., *in the Gospel Call.*

H. L. MENCKEN, in describing a philosopher, un-
willingly but perfectly painted himself; and he
exposed his intellectual nakedness with such indecency that it is a question whether sending it
through the mails does not violate the postal
laws as much as some of his other publications.
Mencken has been to the zoo and felt at home.

THE REV. JAMES H. SNOWDEN, D.D., *in the
Presbyterian Banner.*

H. L. MENCKEN is the Jim Reed of literary
America. The permanent, far-reaching accom-
plishments of this august literary Kaiser, who
hates marriage as much as the earlier Brigham
Young loved it, will be few.

THE REV. F. C. TUCKER, D.D., *of Mexico, Mo.*

THE MENCKEN idea that nobody is any good
except " people who do as I do " is a great detri-
ment to friendship.

THE REV. RICHARD ASPINALL, D.D., *of Terra
Alta, W. Va.*

I BOLDLY declare my lingering though at times flickering faith that he is a better fellow than some people think. The main trouble with Mencken is in his head and not in his heart. He has a moderately good heart, but a woefully weak head.

THE REV. JOHN ROACH STRATON, D.D.

H. L. MENCKEN is the drowning king of darkness.

THE REV. E. SCOTT FARLEY, D.D., *of Suffield, Conn.*

As AN offering to Lewis' god, Mencken, " Elmer Gantry " is poor, but the gracious Mencken accepts it because it reeks with the smell of things which both the god and worshiper like.

THE REV. C. S. SPARKS, D.D., *of Sauk Center, Minn.*

MENCKEN? MENCKEN? I never heard of him, but he's just some cheap jack who's trying to get a reputation by attacking me.

THE REV. BILLY SUNDAY, D.D.

Counter-Offensive

THE CRITICISMS of H. L. Mencken and Sinclair
Lewis are gibbering utterances. They are alone
in their efforts to tide human progress through
the methods observed by Rotary.

> S. WADE MARR, *Governor of the North Carolina
> district of Rotary.*

I do not believe that all the iconoclastic mouthings of H. L. Mencken can weigh as feathers
against the gold of a single, little, undernour-
ished, underprivileged or crippled child, made
happier by the work of the Lions.

> PROFESSOR ERNEST C. MARRINER, *of Colby
> College, Waterville, Maine.*

H. L. MENCKEN, editor of the *American Mercury,* is a notorious writer, the idol of the earthly,
sensual, devilish elements of our country.

> THE ANTI-SALOON LEAGUE OF VIRGINIA.

THE FAITH of Christian Endeavor is simple, sound and firm, and those who hear the sacred songs, religious talks and lectures over the radio are not worrying about the gallery cracks of Henry Mencken.

> MARY RENNELS, *in the Cleveland Press.*

I WONDER if H. L. Mencken and Sinclair Lewis ever recollect that in ridiculing the ideals of Rotary Clubs they are ridiculing the ideals of the Man of Galilee.

> HENRY CLARK, *to the East St. Louis Rotary Club.*

I TAKE no great risk of a libel suit when I state that no slacker ever slacked, and no quacker ever quacked, more or louder than H. L. Mencken, the great foe of Prohibition and friend of " personal liberty."

> L. W. CUNNINGHAM, *in the Colorado Springs Gazette.*

Mr. MENCKEN's chiropractic article would make Iago grin with satisfaction and Othello weep, but our occupation has not gone and long after present orthodox fads have had their day spines will still be subject to subluxations and chiropractors will be rendering a real service to humanity.

"DR." E. E. S. MACKENZIE, *in the Beloit (Wis.) Independent.*

DID MENCKEN ever write, as does the *Rotarian Magazine,* in love and kindliness toward mankind? Rather he has won fame as the national itch.

DONALD ALLAN FARR, *in Public Relations.*

MENCKEN CALLS upon his store of greenish scum to besmatter Mississippi, but the Mississippi press manages to stay above the level of the Mencken sewer just the same; Mississippi churches are pointing men to the stars, while

Mencken points them to the gutter. He is a cynic — clever in some sort of diseased, perverted, moron way — a half-ghoul — a critic of his country, a critic of the South, a critic of the church, a critic of mankind and everything decent, true and pure and good.

The Meridian (Miss.) Star.

THE ROTARIANS are not in the least disturbed over these attacks of Sinclair Lewis and Mencken because the majority of them have never heard of Mencken. These literary poseurs mean little in the lives of the 100% Rotarians.

ALEXANDER McFARLAND, *director of Rotary International.*

MENCKEN IS a dead soul, and to be pitied. There are things he doesn't know and simply can't understand, because he isn't built for knowledge or understanding. It was that spirit which yesterday prompted the city to turn out in masses to greet the visiting Knights Templar, here in splendid observance of Ascension Day. Had H. L. Mencken and his kindred muck-rakers sought the hospitality of the city to exemplify their philosophy of filth, an irate citizenry would have drummed them out of town.

LISSA CLABAUGH, *in the Mattoon (Ill.) Journal-Gazette.*

H. L. MENCKEN is merely venting his sulphurous spleen against America to please his brewery overlords, the majority of whom are now, or have been within two years, under charges of criminal acts. Buzzards only befoul their own nests and there are too many buzzards in the American nest. If Mr. Mencken really has such a horror of American women, American homes and American children, he is informed that scows are still running back to the sordid slums of Europe.

> *The American Issue (organ of the Anti-Saloon League).*

As A literary critic and magazine writer I admire Mencken, but when it comes to his references to osteopathy he never fails to make a plain ass of himself.

> PROFESSOR ANDREW A. GOUR, *of the Chicago College of Osteopathy.*

H. L. MENCKEN, that huckster of choice bits which everyone is supposed to be amused at, and state that Mencken is a bright fellow and unafraid to speak what he thinks, comes to bat with a long harangue against we yokels out here in the country. What makes the huge boards of trade and elevators in Chicago if not we yokels here and at Gopher Prairie? Who buys Society

Hand clothes, that a large factory may be oper-
ated and page ads inserted in the *Saturday Evening Post?*

The Mendota (Ill.) Bulletin.

MENCKEN is the high prophet of the anti-Ameri-
cans. His open, unqualified, and unmitigated
abuse of America, its traditions, customs, and
ideals, is in many ways the most remarkable
spectacle of the times.

*The Methodist Board of Temperance, Prohibi-
tion and Public Morals.*

THERE is an article by H. L. Mencken which is
the vilest slander of the South and Christian
people that has ever been spewed up from the
slimy sewers of a diseased brain and a putrefied
soul. The Order of Knights of Pythias throughout the world will condemn in unmeasured terms
this wholesale indictment.

The Pythian Herald (Little Rock, Ark.).

THE BEST answer to Mencken, the materialist
and sensualist, is Chautauqua.

The Lyceum Magazine.

MENCKEN IS the American Legion's worst enemy.
He says he welcomed the American Legion when
it was organized. Did he think Americans who
gloried in having been through the fires of the
World War would adopt policies pleasing to
him who boasts that he never even bought a
Liberty bond?

The Iowa Legionaire.

MENCKEN, WHOSE writings are of the Greenwich
Village stripe, and whose favorite targets are
Christian Americanism, the Puritan influence,
and those people whom he contemptuously describes as dwellers in the Bible Belt, has at
length aroused organized opposition. Such per-
sons as Mencken are distinctly a liability in the

community where they live. If Baltimore can free itself from Mencken, it will have done a good work.

The American Standard (Ku Klux).

LIAR! INFIDEL! and dishonor to the high and gallant art of fine literature! This fellow has not only grossly insulted the Christian believers in the Virgin Birth of Christ, but the beautiful and kindly State of old Tennessee as well.

EVA PLAMANDON BYRD, *in the Asheville (N. C.) Citizen.*

WHY LUG in chiropractors and New Thought people? You are wrong! Your slant on life is warped, prejudiced, and ten years astern. Better go on your vacation!

GUY A. HUBBARD, *in the Boston Herald.*

WERE MENCKEN to say anything good about an organization it would injure that organization more than if he were to say something bad. No one minds what Mencken says.

> w. d. LITTLE, *president of the Lions Club, Ada, Okla.*

WHEN H. L. MENCKEN assails the Rotarian of today he is attacking the American people.

> RABBI LOUIS BINSTOCK, *in the Charleston (W. Va.) Gazette.*

IF MENCKEN were to view the comradeship, the good fellowship, and the honest joy that is experienced by Rotary members in their organization he would cease his scathing condemnations. I have a sneaking suspicion that the cause of his. attitude is that he was once turned down for membership by some branch of the organization.

> DR. TULLY C. KNOWLES, *president of the College of the Pacific.*

AN ANIMATED sneer, labelled by its progenitor H. L. Mencken, loses no opportunity for classing

the advocates of the Single Tax with the Socialists, Prohibitionists, and adherents to various
isms. Profoundly ignorant of economic laws;
shallow, bumptious, arrogant and insolent, by
dint of iteration of a few shopworn phrases
Mencken has succeeded in getting a following
among the educated boobery that is unable to
distinguish between knowledge and pretense.
Bluff, bluster, and a facility for calling names
constitute the Mencken stock-in-trade.

The Single Tax Review.

RESOLVED, BY the Knights of the Ku Klux Klan
of Arkansas, a State which the said Mencken has
slandered as " a land of morons," that we condemn in the strongest possible language the
vile mouthings of this writer, to whom virtue,
patriotism and decency are only a subject upon
which to expend the venom of a poisonous pen,

and that we protest against the calumny as too degrading and false to come from the heart of one who is not himself a moral pervert.

The Little Rock Democrat.

WHAT HAS Mencken ever said, or done, that lived 30 days? The greatest blessing that can come to the movies is Mencken's fault-finding with them.

A. M. BOWLES, *in the San Francisco Bulletin.*

TENNESSEE HAD an unpalatable taste of this literary mountebank when he appeared at Dayton when the Scopes trial was on and disappeared in what is reported to have been goodly time for the welfare of his cutaneous covering.

The Chattanooga Times.

MINNESOTA MAY have produced no statesmen, poets or painters, according to the estimate of

this would-be iconoclast. But thank God, the State has *never* produced a Mencken!
The Minneapolis Star.

H. L. MENCKEN, whose name indicates that he is of Teutonic extraction, if not actually a native German, undertakes to analyze and discuss the South. We spare the reader lest we dignify this bitter, scurrilous, South-hating iconoclast.
The Danville (Va.) Register.

FROM THE very first of his career Mr. Mencken has created a bad odor in Virginia. He represents everything that is anathema to Virginians.
The Petersburg Progress-Index.

OKLAHOMA FORTUNATELY is little aware of the Mencken menace. But we regard it our duty to sound a timely warning. His launching of the *Mercury* makes the shout of alarm ever more imperative. Nothing American is safe.
The Muscogee Phoenix.

ONE OF the outstanding freaks, who calls himself a writer, is H. L. Mencken. Not satisfied with putting out stuff that is tinged with indecency, he attempts to belittle the people of a great State like West Virginia!

The Sistersville Review.

Winces of the Galled

WHY SHOULD any one worry over H. L. Mencken's strictures? Who ever gave him a license to be a critic?

> PETER B. KYNE, *in the Los Angeles Examiner.*

HE IS violent, impudent, farcical, grotesque and intellectually unscrupulous. It is impossible that writers who " go on " with the pen as he does could reliably distinguish a good book or a good play from a bad one. True taste in literature would have prevented his rabid performances. He makes me laugh as much as a musical absurdity at the Coliseum. Indeed, his proper place is the music-hall.

> ARNOLD BENNETT, *in the London Standard.*

HE WAS born, one can't help thinking, with a predilection for beer and brass chandeliers and fly-specks on the ceiling.

> LOUIS BROMFIELD, *in the Bookman.*

SUCH LANGUAGE as Mencken's is a reminder that words and sentences have frequently been employed by men suffering from auto-intoxication who indulge in statements more dishonest than are told in pictures caught in the eye of the camera and represented on the screen.

REX BEACH, *in the New York Telegraph.*

MENCKEN NEVER knew anything about poetry, and never will.

CLEMENT WOOD, *in the New York Graphic*

SAINT-SAËN's great symphonic poems are not to be sneered at. I do not know any one who disagrees with me except Mencken, whose credo is that if a composer is a German he must not be sneered at, and if a Frenchman he must not be praised.

HENRY T. FINCK, *in the New York Evening Post.*

Mr. Mencken's political and editorial responsibilities, the many bees in his bonnet that have nothing remotely to do with any kind of literature, have prevented him from studying with sufficient earnestness contemporary English letters.

HUGH WALPOLE, *in the Nation (London).*

H. L. Mencken is but a passing fancy.

HAMLIN GARLAND, *in the Waterloo (Iowa) Courier-Reporter.*

Mr. Mencken is beset with the idea that there are only two or three outstanding lights in the literary world today. Mencken is one of them, but he can't remember who the others are.

IRVIN S. COBB, *in the Savannah Press.*

Mencken's is a mind not to be ranked with the De la Mares, Montagues, Santayanas, Tomlinsons. It is a mind obviously and inescapably literal, businesslike, bourgeois. It falls, in broad classification, in the same region with that of Dr. Frank Crane. Dr. Crane is beneath Mencken in only one respect: that the Doctor rarely meddles with topics beyond his reach.

CHRISTOPHER MORLEY, *in the New York Evening Post.*

HE KNOWS nothing about poetry, and he is as boastful of it as any small town bench bum.

GENEVIEVE TAGGARD, *in the Laughing Horse.*

H. L. MENCKEN has at times said unkind things about the English literati of our time. But does he really believe for one moment that any English writer of consequence would have dared to put out a book so shallow, so slick, so innocent of argument and so empty of everything else, as this volume of his entitled " Notes on Democracy " ? If he does he is wrong. There is on every page some misconception.

> REBECCA WEST, *in the New York Herald Tribune.*

MR. AIKEN has proved more effective than Mr. Mencken because in the first place he is an artist, which Mr. Mencken is not in any sense or medium; he is always honest, however misguided; and never vulgar, and he has, whatever his limitations, an intellectual self-respect of the meaning of which Mr. Mencken has not the remotest idea.

> WILLIAM STANLEY BRAITHWAITE, *in the Boston Transcript.*

ONE IS obliged to assume an incapacity in Mencken to handle major ideas. One is also forced to decide that he has very little æsthetic sensibility and no æsthetic understanding whatever.

> GORHAM B. MUNSON, *in the Guardian (Philadelphia).*

ALL WE get from him are Mephistophelian quips and grimaces at whatever earnest striving there is among men.

DR. FRANK CRANE.

I DIMLY remember having read, in the lounge of a Naples hotel, a bit of an article by a Mr. Mencken in German, in some German periodical; all amounting to nothing.

D. H. LAWRENCE, *in the Dial.*

The Voice of the Motherland

I FIND Mr. Mencken full of cocksure inadequacy.
HERBERT READ, *in the New Age.*

A CHILD of the chautauqua.
R. ELLIS ROBERTS, *in the London Daily News.*

IT IS difficult to understand how one so ignorant of English should have been allowed by an American publisher to mislead his country-people — for most American publishers come to England at least once a year.
The Publishers' Circular (London).

MENCKEN HAS absorbed a sham-comedy, swash-bucklering style in some back-water of provincial journalism. English is understood in the four corners of the globe, but Mr. Mencken's comic cuts are merely doleful for people whose patois is not the same as his.
B. S., *in the Manchester Guardian.*

WHEN A child put its fingers to its nose, the act was called " making a snoot," and it was said to be done " on " the person toward whom it was directed. Making snoots on teacher was piquant, dangerous, daring and easy. The phrase exactly describes Mr. Mencken's intellectual attitude.

The New Statesman.

I NEVER expected to meet any one so squat, a veritable tweedledum.

LLEWELYN POWYS, *in the Buffalo Times.*

MR. MENCKEN has no humor. His " In Defense of Women " is absurd, violent and inhuman.

The Saturday Review (London).

HE IS one of those Americans who have an un-erring instinct, improved upon by a lifetime of practice, for tramping on corns.

The Glasgow Herald.

BLOW THE froth off Mencken and you get Shaw;
skim the scum off Shaw and you get Nietzsche;
drain off the lees and settlings of Nietzsche's
melancholy brain and you get Schopenhauer.

FLORENCE BAVERSTOCK, *in the Sydney
(N. S. W.) Bulletin.*

MR. MENCKEN is a Baltimore journalist whose
writing has all the characteristics of the American yellow press. It relies much upon titles, as
the newspaper relies upon headlines. It speaks
with confidence and decision from half-knowl-
edge or complete ignorance.

The Aberdeen (Scotland) Journal.

A ROARING and bellowing democrat. The clown
of an intellectual pantomime, who, while he
merely clouts Pantaloon and touches up the
policeman with his red-hot poker, sees himself
as Lucifer dismantling Heaven.

J. B. PRIESTLEY, *in the London Daily News.*

Prejudices? yes! This is the correct name for these effusions. They become as ridiculous as the small boy who runs along the street kicking every door that he passes.

The Nottingham Journal.

𝔐iscellaneous 𝔈legancies

H. L. MENCKEN, instead of taking a page
ad like the piles cure manufacturers or the fly
paper venders or the corn plaster makers, simply
says something sufficiently shocking or silly to be
quoted.

The Nashville Tennessean.

THE ONLY difference between Mencken and the
man who every time he opened his mouth put
his foot into it is that every time Mencken opens
his he puts both in — and most of the time he
has been wandering around in much muck.

The Harrisburg (Pa.) Telegraph.

DIONYSUS SITTING on a piece of fly-paper.

The Chicago Literary Times.

ANY REASONABLE man's opinion of the latest
abortion of a mind wallowing in a self-created

atmosphere of filthy literary stench which stifles susceptibility to truth and blinds observation of fact, was capably expressed in the editorial columns of the Jackson *Daily News* a few days ago, in reply to the unwarranted accusations of cynical, putrid-souled H. L. Mencken.

The Mississippian (University of Mississippi).

IF A buzzard had laid an egg in a dunghill and the sun had hatched a thing like Mencken, the buzzard would have been justly ashamed of its offspring.

THE REV. CHARLES E. JONES, D.D., *in the Gospel Call.*

MOIST WITH the unpleasant odor of his philological perspiration.

THORNWELL HAYNES, *in the Asheville Citizen.*

WHAT A breath!

WALTER S. HANKEL, *in Aesthete 1925.*

Verdicts in Brief

A TAVERN brawler, drunk on adjectives.

The Nashville Tennessean.

THE BILIOUS buffoon from Baltimore.

PROFESSOR HOWARD DARE WHITE, *to the Jersey City Kiwanis Club.*

HELENMARIA MENCKEN. H. Chaste Mencken. Monsieur Henri La-la-la Ménckène.

PROFESSOR ROBERT C. BROOKS, *of Swarthmore.*

THE MONARCH of saturnalia.

The Daily (University of Minnesota).

THIS EUROPHOBIAC from Maryland might, with no little appropriateness, be referred to as a Baltimoron. He is the field marshal of the Marylandsturm.

The New York Herald Tribune.

AN AFFECTED ass.

EXPURGATORIUS, *in the Johnstown (Pa.) Ledger.*

As uncouth as the ordinary pork butcher.

T. A. B., *in the St. Paul News.*

The megaphonic Barnum of contemporary criticism.

C. J. H., *in the Charlotte (N. C.) Observer.*

Jonathan Edwards in the habiliments of Rabelais.

W. W. robinson, *in the Los Angeles Times.*

An unsavory creature, putrid of soul.

The Venice (Calif.) Vanguard.

The Lenin of critics.

The Bristol (Conn.) Press.

Mencken may be a literati — he's also a damn fool.

The Mendota (Ill.) Bulletin.

The greatest faker and ballyhoo artist of our time. A national menace.

The Muskogee (Okla.) Times-Democrat.

A PUBLIC nuisance.

> *The New York Commercial.*

A LITERARY stink-pot.

> *The Raleigh (N. C.) Times.*

HE REMINDS me of three things: cheap perfume, a headache, and the sound of an ice-wagon going over rough stones.

> M. G. SHELLEY, *in the Baltimore Evening Sun.*

A SMART Aleck who has become a member of Phi Beta Kappa.

> *Hearst's Chicago Herald-Examiner.*

A ONE-STUNT actor.

> *The Nyack (N. Y.) Journal.*

THE VERBOSE Diogenes of Baltimore.

> ROY TEMPLE HOUSE, *in the Oklahoman (Oklahoma City).*

OUR GREATEST heavy-weight of light thinkers.

> GIFO G. EVERETT, *in the Norfolk (Va.) Ledger-Dispatch.*

A MEMBER of the knothole brigade.

The Wichita (Kansas) Eagle.

A LITERARY back-fence gossip.

The Lyceum Magazine.

THE MOST higly-paid common scold in the country.

The Harrisburg (Pa.) Telegraph.

A MISCHIEVOUS bladder-banger.

JAKE FALSTAFF, *in the Akron (O.) Journal.*

MENCKEN HIMSELF is sufficient reason for anything that may be said about him.

The Philadelphia Inquirer.

THE MOST egocentric man that ever lived.

PROFESSOR EDWIN MIMS, *of Vanderbilt University.*

A SCRIBBLER plethoric and thinker vacuous.

The Memphis Commercial-Appeal.

A DAMPHOOL.

The Winter Haven (Fla.) Chief.

AN INSUFFERABLE excrescence on the body of American literature. Even Sing Sing and Matteawan would be contaminated by such as he.

The Little Rock (Ark.) Trade Record.

THE HIGH prophet of the latrine school of writers, who look to the sewers for inspiration.

MAJOR FREDERICK PALMER, *in the American Legion Monthly.*

THE PRIZE pan artist of modern literature.

Motion Pictures Today.

HERR HEINRICH Ludwig Mencken, *Schnarrenmeister und Krebsbruder.*

Stuff and Nonsense (Bryn Athyn, Pa.).

THE MOST monumental egoist ever created by an American transplantation of Prussianism.

BEVERLEY N. SPARKS, *in the Centreville (Md.) Observer.*

A CINDERELLA with flat feet.

The New Republic.

THE LEADING literary fraud of the age.

The Bridgeport (Conn.) Telegram.

THE WORLD'S champion hog-calling ballyhoo boy.

The Richmond Times-Dispatch.

THE MARAT of the Greenwich Village revolution.

JAMES WEBER LINN, *in the Chicago Examiner.*

H. L. MENCKEN'S only claim to fame is that he tries to ape George Bernard Shaw.

The Bridgeport (Conn.) Telegram.

H. L. MENCKEN, the vaudeville critic, is the dominating literary disease. Anti-Victorian in his contempt for virtue, he is ultra-Victorian in his respect for wealth.

V. F. CALVERTON, *in the Sunday Worker (London).*

A SWEET-SCENTED geranium.

> *The Lumberton (N. C.) Robesonian.*

A LITERARY cad.

> LAWRENCE MARTIN, *in the Circle (University of Chicago).*

A DILATED brain impregnated with ego, indigo and gangrene.

> THOMAS J. LITTLETON, *in the Chattanooga News.*

HIS QUALITIES partake strangely of those of the Red Indian in his native state.

> *The Houston Chronicle.*

MENCKEN IS one who functions down in the cellar with the hams and onions.

> *The Philadelphia North American.*

HE MUST have a miserable little shriveled up heart and soul.

> *The Westminster (Md.) Times.*

WE GREET Mencken with disgust.

> *The Grand Rapids (Mich.) Herald.*

THANK GOD we have more Nathan Strauses in this country than H. L. Menckens!

The Providence (R. I.) News.

OUR ONE and only successful Olympian sneerer.

K. S., *in the Boston Transcript.*

THE *SUNDAY STAR* costs the regular subscriber about one cent. Mencken's article costs the reader three fifty-thousandths of one cent — and is worth just that.

THOMAS J. BOYLE, *in the Kansas City Star.*

AN IMPORTED scion of German *Schrecklichkeit.*

The Arkansas Writer.

THIS MODERN Attila! This brachycephalous Caliban! The Black Knight of Slander! An intellectual Houyhnhnm!

CLIO HARPER, *in the Arkansas Writer.*

THE BOSS basilisk.

WILLIAM VALENTINE KELLEY, *in the Methodist Review.*

A TEMPEST in a Volstead beer-mug.

> PROFESSOR FRED LEWIS PATTEE, *in "Side-Lights on American Literature."*

A BABE Ruth who attempts to win a World Series with a rubber bat.

> JOSEPH B. HARRISON, *in "A Short View of Menckenism."*

THE PROPHET of the tawdry run of anti-bourgeois liberals.

> V. F. CALVERTON, *in "The Newer Spirit."*

AMERICA'S SOAPBOX orator, street-corner shouter and table thumper.

> BEN HECHT.

IT WOULD hurt him to be decent.

> THE REV. EUCLID PHILLIPS, *in the Baltimore Evening Sun.*

I DOUBT if Mencken has ever given anything save headaches to the American public.

> LEONARD H. KIRKPATRICK, *in the Milwaukee News.*

WHAT HE writes is bilge.

The Memphis Commercial-Appeal.

HE HAS a dirty way of making a living.

The Wheeling (W. Va.) Register.

A SCHOOL-ROOM cut-up.

JOSEPH KENNICOTT HILTON, *in the Des Moines (Iowa) Register.*

A MONUMENTAL jackass. A liar supreme. A bomb-thrower. His loyalty during the late war was questionable.

The Easton (Md.) Star.

A LITERARY two-gun man. An inspired jackass.

The Nashville Tennessean.

MR. MENCKEN talks about truth as if she were his mistress, but he handles her like an iceman.

STUART P. SHERMAN, *in the Bookman.*

MENCKEN, WHO makes a business of flagellating blunderers, is himself one of the grossest and most bare-faced of that tribe. His egotism is colossal.

Hearst's Chicago American.

H. L. MENCKEN is rude and insulting. He might speak of our mental deficiencies with a more restrained tone.

FLORA E. STEVENS, *in the Kansas City Star.*

H. L. MENCKEN would have made a good black-smith.

The Springfield (Ill.) Register.

HE HAS an assassin's desire for blood.

PROFESSOR LEWIS WORTHINGTON SMITH, *of Duke University.*

WHY ALL this fuss over Herr Mencken? An engaging old dear, amusingly misanthropic, his stuff has all the deadly kick contained in a glass of sarsaparilla.

The Chicago Tribune.

THE BRASH young David who, with five dirty stones such as he can find in any drain, demolishes the Goliaths of our day.

Hearst's Chicago Examiner.

A BALTIMORE Babbitt.

O. O. MCINTYRE.

Soli Deo gloria!

A NOTE
ON THE TYPE
IN WHICH THIS BOOK IS SET

This book is composed on the Linotype in Bodoni, so-called after its designer, Giambattista Bodoni (1740–1813) a celebrated Italian scholar and printer. Bodoni planned his type especially for use on the more smoothly finished papers that came into vogue late in the eighteenth century. Characteristics that will be noted are the square serifs without fillet and the marked contrast between the light and heavy strokes.

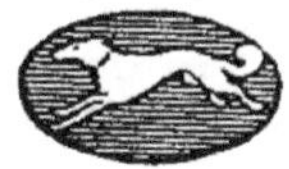

SET UP, ELECTROTYPED, PRINTED
AND BOUND BY
THE PLIMPTON PRESS
NORWOOD · MASS.
PAPER FURNISHED BY W. F.
ETHERINGTON & CO.
NEW YORK